The Path Seekers

ALAA ELSAYED

The Path Seekers

First published in Malaysia by
Tertib Publishing
23-2 Jalan PJS 5/30
Petaling Jaya Commercial City (PJCC)
46150 Petaling Jaya, Selangor
Malaysia

Tel: +603 7772 3156

First Edition: December 2019

Cataloguing in-Publication Data is available from the National Library of Malaysia

ISBN: 978-967-17402-7-9

Cover design: Zahin Zulkipli | www.zahinzul.com
Typesetting & Layout: Ainul Syuhada
Printed by: Firdaus Press Sdn. Bhd.

Contents

Introduction

This is a summary of a beautiful garden of two books: *Manazil As-Sairin* (by Imam Al-Harawi) and *Madarij As-Salikin* (by Ibn Al-Qayyim). We are going to take some of the fruits and flowers from the two books in a nutshell, so we can all be guided. It is all around verse 5 of surah Al-Fatihah, "Only You we worship and only You (O Allah) we seek assistance (for us to be able to worship You)."

We ask Allah s.w.t to give us the ability to be a part of the path seekers. With that, there has some rules and regulations. To be among the path seekers, first thing the scholars will tell you is, "Those who know themselves, he will know Allah s.w.t."

In order to seek knowledge, you have to have taqwa. Allah s.w.t mentions that if you have piety, He will grant you knowledge.

"... And fear Allah, and Allah teaches you ..."
(Surah Al-Baqarah, verse 28)

Imam Ash-Shafie *rahimahullah* said, "The knowledge of Allah s.w.t is not going to be given to the disobedient slaves." Therefore, the rules and regulations are very crucial.

In surah Al-Kahf verse 103, Allah s.w.t says,

"Say [O Muhammad], 'Shall we inform you of the greatest losers as to (their) deeds? (They are) those whose effort is lost in worldly life, while they think they are doing well in work.'"

That is what mentioned in surah Al-Fatihah, verse 7, "The path of those upon whom You have bestowed favor, not of those who have evoked (Your) anger or of those who are astray." Think about it. Allah s.w.t gets angered with those who have the knowledge but they do not put into practice. And those who have been led astray means that those who are doing actions and deeds with no knowledge. These two ways are what we have to think about. If you have the knowledge, you have to implement it and also you cannot do the deeds without acquiring the knowledge.

The reason that we are created is that according to what Allah s.w.t says as in surah Adh-Dhariyat, verse 56,

"And I did not create the jinn and mankind except to worship Me."

The jinn are those who are unknown or unseen, but they are still be accountable for. Thus, both the jinn and human beings are created to worship Allah s.w.t.

Allah s.w.t says,

"And whoever turns away from My remembrance, indeed he will have a depressed life ..." (Surah Ta Ha, verse 124)

It means that those who stay away from what Allah s.w.t has revealed in the Quran and stay away from the sunnah of Prophet Muhammad s.a.w, will have difficulties in life. No matter how rich you are, you are still poor; no matter how much status or power you gain, you are still weak; and so on and so forth. There is a void in your heart that you do not have the satisfaction, and there is always something that you feel worry about.

In this life, there are some people you want to follow and there are some people you want to stay away from. The scholars say, "There are among the people, they know that they are knowledgeable and they know that they know; so follow him. Then there are those who are knowledgeable but they don't know they are knowledgeable; they are the heedless, so wake them up. Then there are among the people who don't know and they know that they don't know; so teach them. And among the people, there are those who have no knowledge and they don't know that they don' know; that is the shaytan, so avoid them."

Allah s.w.t gives us a fact,

"And (by) the soul and He who proportioned it. And inspired it (with discernment of) its wickedness and its righteousness. He has succeeded who purifies it. And he has failed who instills it (with corruption)." Surah Ash-Shams, verses 7-10.

Most of us know what to do and what not to do. It feels right and it feels wrong. But it is the behavior that we have to change. We have to change in order to be on the straight path.

We have a control over our car; we can drive it around the city or to a nice place. But when we are in the driving seats and our GPS says that if we take this route, we will end up here and if we take that route, we will end up there. We make the decision of which route we want to choose. It is the same thing with life. Allah s.w.t has given you the guidance of which way is the right way to go if you want to end up in Jannah. He also has given you the warning of which way that you take that you will end up in Hellfire. Therefore, you should not be surprise of where you will end up when you already knew the consequences.

By His mercy, Allah s.w.t tells us what is waiting for us, what do we have to do; not only what the questions are but also the answers for the questions. However, we must acquire the knowledge.

In this universe, Allah s.w.t grants us so much to see and to ponder upon. He also gives us the mind that we use to reflect upon His creation. For example, Allah s.w.t gives us the eyesight or vision. However, without the light, the eyes are useless. That means we need the light in order for us to be able to see with the eyes. So it is the same thing – we need to have the mind and intellect in order for us to ponder and reflect. In addition, we must have knowledge so that we can use our mind in a proper manner.

The iman increases and decreases. It increases with the good deeds and it decreases with sins. Therefore, if you want your iman to increase, you have to do more righteous deeds. To have your iman decreases is also an option that you will decide on your own, which is when you sin.

According to Ibn Taymiyyah, nothing is worth upon sins because you pay the price for it both here and in the hereafter. Al-Ghazali said that knowledge of Allah s.w.t is among the great things and the fruit of it is something that you really need to understand its value and its magnitude.

The scholars say that there are various stages of iman that is increases and decreases. First, iman that does not increase nor decreases, which is faith of the angels. Second, iman that only increase and does not decrease, which is faith of the prophets. For the believers, no matter our iman increases or decreases, we have to stay on the straight path.

The scholars also say that if you act upon what you have learned, Allah s.w.t will grant you the knowledge of that what you know not of. Therefore, we have to acquire the knowledge in order for us to gain more benefit.

There is a hadith that mentioned purification is half of faith. There are four stages and understanding of this. First, you purify the body from any impurities. Next, you have to purify the soul from any illness of the heart. Then, you have to purify the eyes, ears, and all senses from the active disobedience. And your heart has to be purified from the illness of shirk. In surah At-Tawbah, verse 111, Allah s.w.t says,

> "Indeed, Allah has purchased from the believers their lives and their properties (in exchange) for that they will have Paradise. ..."

In this verse, the word "their lives" was mentioned first before "their properties". And Paradise is the fruit. Indeed, the merchandise and the commodity of Allah s.w.t is Paradise. In order for us to have this trade with Allah s.w.t, we have to purify our heart, soul, and mind.

To acquire knowledge, we must free ourselves from the imprisonment of the desire. The scholars say, you will face difficulties when you want to do the act of obedience. But know that the difficulties is temporary and the reward for it is eternal. If you do the act of disobedience, the pleasure of it is temporary and will be gone, and what is left is the record of this disobedience. Therefore, you have to be wise about the decision you make in life.

Imam Ash-Shafie said, "I was walking at the Kaabah and I heard a man said, 'O Allah, be pleased with me!'" So he asked the man, "Are you please with Allah, before Allah s.w.t pleases with you?" Whatever Allah s.w.t has given you, they are equal. When hardship be brought to you and you accept because the decree comes from Allah s.w.t, that means you are please with Allah. And Allah s.w.t will be pleased with you.

There is a dua that we can recite: *Allahumma anta maqsudi, wa ridaka matlubi* "O Allah, You are my ultimate goal and Your pleasure is what I seek."

For thirteen years, Prophet Muhammad s.a.w said, "Say there is only one deity deserves to be worshiped, which is Allah. And you will be prosperous in this world and in the hereafter." In the Makkan era, the first message is knowing Allah s.w.t. "Know Allah s.w.t before you know His command." It is important to know and understand why do we have to do the act of worship. If we know Allah s.w.t and the reward from worshiping Him, we want to do everything for Him and we will live our lives for Him.

Thereafter, in the Madinan era, it is about what to do and what not to do. Once people know Allah s.w.t and have tawheed, it is easier to act on what is right and to leave what is wrong. That is also why Muslims become happy in the month of Ramadan. The scholars say that the Muslims are happy in the month of Ramadan because they are doing what they were created to do. In surah Adh-Dhariyat verse 56, Allah s.w.t says,

> "And I did not create the jinn and mankind except to worship Me."

The question for us to reflect now is as mentioned in surah Al-Hadid verse 16,

> "Has the time not come for those who have believed that their hearts should become humbly submissive at the remembrance of Allah ..."

"HAS THE TIME NOT COME FOR THOSE WHO HAVE BELIEVED THAT *their hearts* SHOULD BECOME HUMBLY SUBMISSIVE AT *the remembrance of Allah* ..."

02

Seeking Knowledge

Seeking knowledge is one of the many levels of coming close to Allah s.w.t. According to the scholars, this is one of the highest levels because Allah s.w.t told Prophet Muhammad s.a.w,

> "... O Allah, increase my knowledge." (Surah Ta Ha, verse 114)

The verse does not mention "increase my wealth" or "increase my health" or any other else. The scholars say that if you want to ask Allah s.w.t to increase anything in your life, ask to increase your knowledge. It is because the knowledge is like the imam or the leader, and the practice is like the followers.

Rules and regulations are important in order to stay on the path seekers. If you do an action or deed with no knowledge, this is among the Insanity. Meanwhile, it is simply wrong if you have the knowledge and you do absolutely nothing.

Knowing that, the key to knowledge is taqwa. Allah s.w.t says,

> "... And fear Allah, and Allah teaches you ..." (Surah Al-Baqarah, verse 28)

This is the key. Now let's look on the path. How did Prophet Muhammad s.a.w get onto this path by Allah s.w.t? The Prophet s.a.w received a vision for six months. He would see something in his dreams and it will come true the following day. By sending the vision, Allah s.w.t was preparing him to receive the knowledge. This is the first stage.

The second stage was the first word in the Quran – as we all know – *Iqra'*. Recite, acquire knowledge. Allah s.w.t is telling us through Prophet Muhammad s.a.w, "If you want to be on that path, you have to do that – recite, acquire knowledge." That is the reason why Allah s.w.t says,

> "The Most Merciful. Taught the Quran." (Surah Ar-Rahman, verses 1-2)

How amazing. First, Allah s.w.t says *ArRahman* – one of His attributes. Next, He says what He does – taught the Quran. Follows by the third verse, "Created man". Usually, if you use your logic, you will mention about created the human being then taught them the Quran. But in surah ArRahman, Allah s.w.t shows that the knowledge comes before the creation. The importance for us to seek this path is the reason we were created. Therefore, Allah s.w.t puts emphasis first on the knowledge. Without knowledge, human beings will be totally lost. Without knowledge, we have no path to follow.

It is important for us to know that acquiring knowledge is not easy. We must have zeal for it. We must have taqwa, sincerity, commitment, and patience. When you choose to be on the path of knowledge, do not look back. Have you ever seen a scholar looked back? Look forward and keep going. Let other people talk and do whatever they wish to talk and do. Do not let anybody take you down.

There are two types of students in the path of knowledge. Either you are a student that happen to be a Muslim or a Muslim that happens to be a student. Which one are you? And why do you acquire knowledge? To show-off? There is a hadith that mentions about this matter. It says that Allah s.w.t will ignite fire for three types of people; one of them is for those who seek knowledge so that others will praise them.

What does it mean when you are a student that happens to be a Muslim? "Islam does not mean much to me, I'm just doing this as my priority to acquire the knowledge of this worldly life." This is not a forbidden thinking. However, how can we change that into an act of worship? Do not let the acts of worship to become something as a cultural or habit or something as traditional. But let everything you know in life to be an act of worship, with the intention. For example, you seek knowledge with the intention to bring back the ummah to the front again. In everything that we do in life, if we can make a sincere intention to Allah s.w.t, He will accept from us.

The scholars encourage us to make sincere intention to Allah s.w.t in everything that we do, even when are going to sleep. "I want to get some sleep so I will be able to worship You, o Allah." "I acquire knowledge so I can be a great Muslim example." Therefore, seeking knowledge should come with sincere intention for Allah s.w.t.

The third stage is where Allah s.w.t told Prophet Muhammad s.a.w,

"Arise (to pray) the night, except for a little-"
(Surah Al-Muzzammil, verse 2)

The scholars say that the key for knowledge is taqwa. Taqwa is you being pray in front of Allah when there is no one else around. In Ramadan, we learn about taqwa as mentioned in the Quran; that we fast to attain taqwa. What is holding you back is not eating behind the closed door. You can eat and drink as you wish because nobody else sees you. However, you do not do that because you realize Allah s.w.t sees you.

What is the relation between praying at night and seeking knowledge? The knowledge that you acquire will have to be put into action. Umar ibn Al-Khattab (*may Allah be pleased with him*) said, "We learned the knowledge and action together."

The fourth stage is what Allah s.w.t mention in surah Al-Muddaththir, verse 2,

"Arise and warn."

Imam Malik (*may Allah has mercy on him*) said, "Go and speak when you don't want to sleep. But don't sleep when you want to speak." What does this mean? Once you have acquired the knowledge, then only you talk because at that time you will know the responsibility that is bestowed upon you by Allah s.w.t.

Prophet Muhammad s.a.w said, "If you lie upon me knowingly or intentionally, you can choose your place in the Hellfire." This shows the importance of acquiring the knowledge in stages. When you acquire knowledge but you don't want to talk, you can still talk. But without knowledge, you are not supposed to talk about the issue. It is the right for everyone.

So the stages of path of knowledge of Prophet Muhammad s.a.w begins with vision, follow by recite, then put the knowledge into action, and warn the people.

Allah s.w.t says in surah At-Tahrim, verse 6,

"O you who have believed, protect yourselves and your families from a Fire ..."

First you protect yourself, and then your family. After that, work your way out. And then be patient unto your Lord because the path of knowledge is not easy. Think about the difficulties that the prophets and the messengers have to go through. Prophet Nuh a.s gave dawah for 950 years and only few people followed him. The prophets and the messengers taught us to stay firm.

When you start seeking the knowledge, the first thing you are going to go through is you will be conceited. "I learn from this course", "I learn from that shaykh", "I read this book", "I went to this place to learn this". You will become arrogant.

That is why the scholars say the more you acquire knowledge, the more you fear Allah. "Indeed, the one that actually fear Allah is the one who acquire full knowledge." Scholars cry and feel anxious because they have reached so high and they are afraid to fall and go astray. The scholars are like trees; the more they give their fruits and what they have on their branches, the branches will come down. This is tawaduk. If you humble yourself in front of Allah s.w.t, Allah will raise your rank up.

If you are going to acquire knowledge, Allah s.w.t will grant you more than you think. It is because of the hadith that says that those who seek the path of knowledge, Allah s.w.t will pave their way to Jannah.

Basically, we need knowledge to do everything in this life. Prophet Muhammad s.a.w had mentioned in so many ahadith that he asked us to follow the

Quran and sunnah, take from his examples. Al-Junaid, among the ulama said, "Every path in this worldly life if you want to go to Allah, is closed except that which you follow the footsteps of Prophet Muhammad s.a.w."

Even Umar ibn Al-Khattab (*may Allah be pleased with him*) said, "This is the Messenger of Allah. Follow his footsteps."

The next thing you are going to go through and you must know while in the path of knowledge is tawaduk. Tawaduk is humbleness. You do not walk into a mosque and challenge people to ask you question, just because you have acquire some knowledge. This is not humbleness.

Then it is ignorance. The scholars say, "The more you know, the more that you know you don't know." While preparing their material to teach, some of my teachers realize that there are still a lot of things they don't know. Knowledge is an ocean, subhanallah. In this case, how do you preach to others? Allah s.w.t says in surah Ibrahim, verse 4,

"And we did not send any messenger except (speaking) in the language of his people to state clearly for them."

Not just the language literally, but also understanding their mentality, the environment, what makes them to do something, and how to acquire their love.

We should not be like people who tell others, "Everything is haram", "Everyone is going to Hellfire", and things like this. Prophet Muhammad s.a.w would be sad if he know this is what the students of knowledge do.

Also, don't forget to smile. Being a religious leader or an imam does not necessarily mean you have to show serious or stern face all the time. Smile because it is an act of charity. Touch people's heart so that they will listen to you.

Then you educate with hikmah. Invite people to the path of Allah with good language. Prophet Muhammad s.a.w invited Umar Al-Khattab to Islam with Umar's language, which is power. The Messenger of Allah s.a.w grabbed Umar's shoulder and said, "Isn't it time for you to become a Muslim, o Umar?"

Therefore, it is important to know the people's mind and their key language and touch their heart to get them to listen to you. You must also have patience while teaching knowledge just as you need the patience in seeking knowledge. This is how you enjoin the heart.

The Messenger of Allah s.a.w advised us to first give people what is halal or what is right. Maybe a person does not know what is right and what is wrong, what is permissible and what is impermissible. This is when we educate them using the knowledge that we acquire and we educate with hikmah or wisdom. We have to also acknowledge the etiquette of being able to discuss issues that are khilaf. For example, when it comes to the time of moon sighting for Ramadan. People without knowledge shall see how those who have the knowledge handle this matter.

After you educate people on what is halal or right, then you can tell them about what is haram or wrong or impermissible in Islam. Tell them the reason so they understand.

Ata ibn Rabah is a student of Abdullah ibn Abbas (*may Allah be pleased to both of them*). Ata ibn Rabah was known for his knowledge. Amirul Mukminin at that time was Sulayman ibn Abdul Malik. He asked, "Who is the most knowledgeable person here?" Everyone said it is Ata ibn Rabah. Sulayman ibn Abdul Malik looked for Ata ibn Rabah and he saw a man who is dark, with curly hair, and with not much possession or wealth. Amirul Mukminin Sulayman asked Ata ibn Rabah, "What honored you of this status?"

Ata ibn Rabah said, "When I actually renounced the world of the people. And the people's need for knowledge."

After Amirul Mukminin Sulayman ibn Abdul Malik listened to this answer, he said, "No one will give fatwa in this country, except Ata ibn Rabah."

Then came the time for hajj and Sulayman ibn Abdul Malik wanted to ask about something he had no knowledge of related to this ritual. So he looked for Ata ibn Rabah. When the Amirul Mukminin saw there were a lot of people around Ata ibn Rabah, he wanted to cut the lines.

Ata ibn Rabah said, "Stay where you are, o Amirul Mukminin. Do not cut these lines."

Amirul Mukminin listened to Ata ibn Rabah and he did not cut the lines. He waited for his turn and when his time arrived, he asked Ata ibn Rabah about what is halal and what is haram about hajj. Then Sulayman ibn Abdul Malik told his children, "By Allah, I never was humbled by anyone, except this man."

That is why when you climb a mountain of knowledge, the higher you go and once you reach at the peak, what do you see? You will have a bigger and broader idea of what is in front of you. You see the whole land. You do not obtuse nor restrict. Therefore, the higher you go in the path of knowledge, Allah s.w.t will raise you as high.

Know that this path of seeking knowledge is the path where the angels will spread their wings for you and Allah s.w.t will pave the way for you to Jannah.

THE KEY FOR

knowledge

IS

taqwa.

03

Taqwa

Allah s.w.t linked taqwa with the month of Ramadan for a reason.

In surah Al-Baqarah verse 183, Allah s.w.t says,

"O you who have believed, decreed upon you is fasting as it was decreed upon those before you that you may become righteous-"

In this chapter, we are going to look at taqwa in different ways; from the verses of the Quran, from the hadith, and from the example of righteous predecessors.

Ali ibn Abi Talib *(may Allah be pleased with him)* said that taqwa is being conscious with Allah s.w.t, establishing the Quran within you and your whole life, being prepared for the Day of Judgment, and many others. Some of the opinions also mentioned that Allah s.w.t should never see you at a place where He forbade you and He should never missed you at a place where He ordains you to be. For example, Allah s.w.t should never see you in the bars, but rather He should see you in the mosques.

Some of the people say even at the time of the pre-Islamic, people would say, "This man (or this woman) has taqwa." It means that they do not speak much. Because the senses – your eyes, ears, your mouth – what you say, what you see, what you hear, what you touch, and everything your limbs desire have to be in-checked.

Now think about your eyes as camera, your ears and mouth as audio player, your mind as a modem, and your heart as the hard drive. Everything you see, say, and hear is downloaded and it will be uploaded on the Day of Judgment. Will you be proud of this recording? You can hide it here, but you will never be able to hide it there.

This is why the scholars tell us that fasting is a secret between you and Allah s.w.t. Think about this – what hold you back from eating when you are all alone? What hold you back from drinking when you are all alone? So how do we learn taqwa from fasting? It is easy. You can fast in front of people; you don't eat and drink in front of people, but as soon as you go home and close all the doors and the only door you open is the door of the fridge, do you have taqwa?

According to the scholars, taqwa breaks the desires and it prepares you to be conscious of Allah s.w.t. What does this mean? It helps you during the day to be conscious of Allah s.w.t because of that secret act of worship. That is why Allah s.w.t says, "Fasting is for Me and I will reward it for you." That is sufficient.

The scholars say, "If you leave something that is halal, how could you do something that is haram?" There is a reason why it is called the School of Ramadan. You learn something about yourself first and the most important of all is taqwa. So the only time you know whether you have taqwa or not is when you are all alone. You will be alone when you die, in the grave, when you hear the question "where is Fulan ibn Fulan? Stop them, they will be asked".

Therefore, when you are conscious of Allah s.w.t when you are all alone, He will help you when no one is around. When Umar ibn Al-Khattab *(may Allah be pleased with him)* heard the verse 24 surah As-Saffat,

"And stop them; indeed, they are to be questioned", he fell ill for a month. People would visit him but he did not know. This is the taqwa that he had attained.

The month of Ramadan is a training for us to leave that which is haram. Prophet Muhammad s.a.w taught us in his tradition, he said, "When someone comes and curses you, you reply with 'I am fasting.'" Ramadan is also a training month to hold back on desires – no talking back, no intimate relations, and no active disobedience. Ramadan is a stage where you learn from it and move on.

The word taqwa has been recorded 240 times in the Quran.

> "... And take provisions, but indeed the best provision is fear of Allah; and fear Me, o you of understanding." (Surah Al-Baqarah, verse 197)

In the above verse, Allah s.w.t says increase of that in your life and the best to increase according to Him is taqwa. Why?

> "And there is none of you except he will come to it; this is upon your Lord an inevitability decreed. Then We will save those who feared Allah and leave the wrongdoers within it, on their knees." (Surah Maryam, verse 71 and 72)

There is no exception here – everyone among us will pass over the Hellfire, on the sirat or bridge. Therefore it is enough for us to attain taqwa from the month of Ramadan, to prepare for that day.

Now imagine this. One day you want to take a break from the month of Ramadan. So you go on the internet and you look for a halal enough vacation package. Then you book it. After that, you get the itinerary and the welcome notes: *Congratulations on your vacation! Here is your itinerary, but there are minor changes. Do not bother packing because you will not need luggage where you are going. This is a one-way ticket and you are not coming back. The pilot is the Angel of Death. Destination: Unknown. Accommodation: Six meters beneath the ground.* How do you feel then? Will you worry about all of the worldly life desires?

Allah s.w.t says,

"The month of Ramadan (is that) in which was revealed the Quran ..."
(Surah Al-Baqarah, verse 185)

Ramadan is the month where Allah s.w.t honored with the Quran. What does that mean?

"This is the book about which there is no doubt,
a guidance for those conscious of Allah."
(Surah Al-Baqarah, verse 2)

Indeed, this is the month that Allah s.w.t revealed the Quran, the scripture that we read all about. If you want to be on the straight path, this is the book. If you want to be protected with your senses and if you want to protect your tongue, use it for tadabbur the Quran. This is also how you attain taqwa. This is the book of guidance of those who are conscious of Allah s.w.t.

Abdullah ibn Abbas *(may Allah be pleased with him)* used to hold his tongue. He said, "Say good that you will be prosperous. And be silent upon any evil, you will be saved. But if you do not do that, then know for sure you will regret."

Some of the scholars say that your ears have no gates, no protection – you hear everything. But there is one layer at the eyes upon what you see – which is the eyelids. And there are two guards before the tongue – the teeth and the lip. This is a reminder for you so that you understand what you are saying.

There is no good of those who has fast when they leave their foods and drinks, but they don't leave backbiting and gossiping and the likes. The meaning of fasting is to break the desires and to prepare your nafs from nafs al-ammarah (evil desire) to nafs al-mutmainnah (soul that is peaceful).

Umar ibn Abdul Aziz *(may Allah be pleased with him)* said, "Taqwa is not fasting during the day and praying during the night. Rather, taqwa is leaving what Allah s.w.t told you to leave and do what He told you to do."

Umar ibn Al-Khattab *(may Allah be pleased with him)* asked Ubay ibn Ka'ab *(may Allah be pleased with him)*, "You teach us about taqwa. What is that?"

Ubay ibn Ka'ab *(may Allah be pleased with him)* replied, "Have you not seen, o Amirul Mukminin, a path that you have taken, there are thorns. What do you do?"

"I will roll up and I will make sure that I put my feet where I will not be harmed."

"That is taqwa."

So from now on, where you are going to take your feet to, or where your eyes are going to look at, or what your ears are going to hear, what your two hands are going to do; they are all evidence of your piety. The most important point is where your heart is going to take you, because taqwa is in the heart. While you are boasting about yourself, Allah s.w.t knows whether you have taqwa or not.

Leave the act of disobedience – small or big – and walk upon the earth as if it is full of thorns. Do not belittle a small act of sin because indeed it can grow bigger. Do not look at the small insignificant sin that you commit, but look at the greatness of The One that you commit sins against.

Abdullah ibn Mubarak *(may Allah has mercy upon him)* said, "If you are conscious of Allah s.w.t in 100 issues, but you are not conscious of Him in one issue, you are not among the muttaqin."

Taqwa is hearing to your subconscious mind. For the muttaqin, they even get to a stage where they leave some of the halal fearing it is haram. This is called *al-warak*.

According to Imam Ahmad ibn Hanbal (*may Allah has mercy upon him*), "Taqwa is leaving that which you desire for that which you conscious of and fear."

One day while Amirul Mukminin, Harun Ar-Rashid (*may Allah be pleased with him*) was walking, a Jewish man said to him, "Fear Allah!" What did Harun Ar-Rashid do thereafter? He got off his ride and he prostrated to Allah s.w.t. He was afraid that he would become one of those people who when it is said to them 'fear Allah!', they tend to do more sins because of their high status and honor.

Abu Bakar As-Siddiq (*may Allah be pleased with him*) used to ask about the food before he ate something. One time, one of his servants brought some food and he forgot to ask him. But after Abu Bakar ate, he asked the servant, "Where did you get this food from, o ghulam?"

The servant said, "From a place where the people see fortune-tellers."

Abu Bakar As-Siddiq *(may Allah be pleased with him)* then place his fingers in his throat and he got the foods out. How amazing that was.

Ask ourselves: How many times have we eaten things that are haram and drink from that is haram? Taqwa is finding out where the money is coming from, what do you eat and drink, what do you wear; every aspect of your life.

Ali ibn Abi Talib *(may Allah be pleased with him)* said, "O dunya, go and see somebody else. Are you beautifying yourself for me? Are you longing for me? I have given you talaq three times. Your lifespan is very short. And this prolonged journey is very little. So I'm not interested in you."

Think about this. How many of us submerse ourselves in the desires we are present for in the worldly life? We are focusing on something that is actually not there.

Hasan Al-Basri *(may Allah has mercy upon him)* said, "Allah s.w.t made the month of Ramadan as a race track where the horses compete. In such a place and time, everyone should be actually competing.

Here you are; those who want to do good, come! And those who want to do bad, stay away from it!"

"... The most noble of you in the sight of Allah is the most righteous of you ..." (Surah Al-Hujurat, verse 13)

ABDULLAH IBN MUBARAK
(MAY ALLAH HAS MERCY UPON HIM)
SAID,
"IF YOU ARE CONSCIOUS OF ALLAH S.W.T IN 100 ISSUES, BUT YOU ARE NOT CONSCIOUS OF HIM IN ONE ISSUE, YOU ARE NOT AMONG THE MUTTAQIN."

04

Sabr
(Patience)

There are three types of sabr or patience:

1. Being patience on the divine decree of Allah s.w.t

2. Being patience upon what Allah s.w.t forbade us to do

3. Being patience upon that which is Allah s.w.t ordains us to do

Patience on the divine decree

Allah s.w.t will test you in different ways. He will take away somebody that is close to your heart and give somebody else in your life that will give you a hard time; or a lost of job; or decrease in health or wealth; or maybe lost of limbs that mean a lot to you. This is divine decree and we must be patient on that.

Patience upon what Allah s.w.t forbade us to do

Do not lie, do not steal, do not cheat, do not fornicate, and everything that is not very easy to do so, but it is among the types of patience.

Patience upon that which is Allah s.w.t ordains us to do

Allah s.w.t orders that you to lower your gaze, to be honest, to pray, to give zakah, and to perform other acts of obedience.

Bonus: Beautiful Patience

The type of patience where you complain to no one, except to Allah s.w.t. The best example of this type of patience is of Ya'qub (a.s).

In surah Al-Baqarah, verse 286, Allah s.w.t says,

"Allah does not charge a soul except (with that within) its capacity ..."

No one is burdened with more than they can handle. That means Allah s.w.t already told you whatever He is going to test you with, you can afford. You will be tested according to your ability and your own measure of iman. The higher the iman, the higher the test.

The highest level of people would have been tested are the prophets and the messengers, and then those with the lower of iman, and so on and so forth. Therefore, be grateful in that essence because Prophet Muhammad s.a.w said, "How wonderful is the affair of the believer, for his affairs are all good. And this applies to no one but the believer. If something good happens to him, he is thankful for it and that is good for him. If something bad happens to him, he bears it with patience and that is good for him." (Recorded by Imam Muslim)

You will be tested in your life. Especially when you live in the west, where people give you bad look, they make fun of your beard or any religious clothing.

In surah Al-Mutaffifin, verse 29 to 31, Allah s.w.t says,

"Indeed, those who committed crimes used to laugh at those who believed. And when they passed by them, they would exchange derisive glances. And when they returned to their people, they would return jesting."

In this verse, Allah s.w.t calls them the criminal. They are those who would make fun of the believers and when they go home, they would make fun of the believers again with their family. That is fine because Allah s.w.t says indeed you are going to go through these steps. And on the Day of Judgment, Allah s.w.t says you will be laughing at them. At which place do you want to laugh? In this worldly life or in the hereafter?

Yes, you are going to go through difficulties. Yes, you are going to get that different look. Yes, they will harm you. But to be patient with all these would be so much better for you. You do not have to burn from inside; let them know this. Say thank you instead.

Allah s.w.t has given us prophets and messengers to be example for us, as well as the example from the pious predecessors. We take Ayyub (a.s) as an example. Allah s.w.t gives him so much, but all of a sudden, he is being tested. He is now bleed with an illness. He cannot do anything and he cannot even move for 18 years. Allah s.w.t has given him children, but all of his children are gone. Now his wife has to work, but nobody wants to give her a job anymore because they are afraid Ayyub's (a.s) illness is contagious. They reach to the point where she has to sell her hair.

Then the wife asks Ayyub (a.s) to ask for Allah's help. Ayyub (a.s) feels shame because the duration of his adversity is too little compared to the duration of ease that Allah s.w.t has bestowed him with. But then he makes dua to Allah. After that, Allah s.w.t granted him double in his children and everything back. It is the reward for his patience.

When Umm Salama's husband died, Prophet Muhammad s.a.w said to her, "Be patient. Say *(Allahumma ajurni fi musibati, wakhluf li khairan minha)* O Allah, reward me in the calamity and grant me with something better."

Abu Salama was among the greatest companions and he had died as a martyr in a battle. When the Prophet s.a.w taught Umm Salama the dua, she asked him, "Who is better than Abu Salama, o Messenger of Allah?" Eventually she married Prophet Muhammad s.a.w.

The story of Umm Salama is beautiful. Abu Salama wanted to migrate with Prophet Muhammad s.a.w. He wanted to take his wife and their child with him. The tribe of Umm Salama said no. They would not allow Abu Salama to bring Umm Salama together to Madinah. Therefore, Abu Salama could only bring their child. Umm Salama then had to separate from his husband and son.

Umm Salama said, "Everyday I would go to the borders of Makkah, from sunrise to sunset and cried until I have no more tears."

Now after a long story, Allah s.w.t bestowed her a marriage with the Messenger of Allah s.a.w, an immense reward. We can learn from Umm Salama how to hold on to patience.

Prophet Ismail (a.s) get married to a woman who has no patience. One day, his father, Ibrahim (a.s) went to visit their house. As soon as Ibrahim (a.s) heard his son's wife complained about everything and she did not content about anything, he said, "Please deliver this message to your husband. Tell him change the step of the door." Basically he meant change your wife.

After Ismail (a.s) got married to a new wife, Ibrahim (a.s) came to visit his son again. When he asked the woman how was everything and their life, she said, "Alhamdulillah, everything is good." Ibrahim (a.s) then asked the woman to deliver the message to his son, "Hold on to your doorstep." Which means keep your wife.

Do not let your wife to be a test for you and do not let your husband to be a test for you either. There is no obedience in the creation if it means disobedience in The Creator.

A disbeliever has everything in his life. True, they can do anything here. The scholars say the life is a prison for a true believer, but it is heaven for a disbeliever. What is waiting for the believer in Jannah cannot be compared with everything in this worldly life. Therefore, we are encouraged to be content with what Allah s.w.t decreed upon us.

> "O you who have believed, seek help with
> patience and prayer."
> Surah Al-Baqarah, verse 153.

Prophet Muhammad s.a.w showed example how he seek comfort in prayer. This is when he asked Bilal bin Rabah *(may Allah be pleased with him)* to make adhan while they were taking a rest from a journey. Also, the righteous company you keep will help you to have that patience among one another.

Allah s.w.t gives the attributes of those who are patience.

"... and (those who) are patient in poverty and hardship and during battle; those are the ones who have been true, and it is those who are the righteous."
(Surah Al-Baqarah, verse 177)

Even in the difficulties and in war, they were still holding on to their patience. They are the one who are truthful with their iman and they attain taqwa through patience.

"And We will surely test you with something of fear and hunger and a loss of wealth and lives and fruits, but give good tidings to the patient."
(Surah Al-Baqarah, verse 155)

"Do the people think they will be left to say, 'We believe' and they will not be tested?"
(Surah Al-Ankabut, verse 2)

It is your choice whether to be patient or to not be patient with the tests from Allah.

> "And as for man, when his Lord tries him and
> (thus) is generous to him and favors him, he
> says, 'My Lord has honored me.' But when He
> tries him and restricts his provision, he says,
> 'My Lord has humiliated me.' No! But you do
> not honor the orphan."
> (Surah Al-Fajr, verses 15-17)

If Allah s.w.t gives a man all the bounties – good job, good spouse, good children, good car, good house, good everything – he will say, "I am the honorable. Allah loves me!" And if Allah restricted his source of provision, he complains, "Oh no! I'm humiliated!"

It is not necessarily only when Allah s.w.t grants you with all the bounties and provisions that He is pleased with you. It could also a bad sign, especially when you are not being content and grateful.

And if Allah deprive you with something, it does not mean that He is dishonoring you. That could be good. Why? Think about this. When do you usually go to Allah s.w.t? When you have a final exam, when you need to get married, when you need that job, when you need to get out of debts, and other types of trials. So we actually have no idea if a trial is good or bad for us.

That is why the scholars say the best dua to recite is: *Rabbana atina fi-ddunya hasanah, wa fi-l akhirati hasanah wa qina 'adhaba annar.* "O Allah, give us the best of life and the best of akhirah, and protect us from Hellfire." This dua is from surah Al-Baqarah, verse 201.

Allah s.w.t has given us a beautiful example. He says those who pardon people and control their anger are among those who excel that attributes. There is a story about a young female servant. One day, she unintentionally poured hot water on her master and he got burnt. When he got angry, she reminded him, "Allah s.w.t gives honor to those who control their anger."

The master said, "I control my anger."

She added, "And those who pardon people."

The master said, "I pardon you."

She added, "And loves those who are excellent in everything that they do."

The master said, "Go, you are now free and you no longer a slave."

When you deal with your children, your spouse, your boss, and others, just remember these: Control your anger, pardon people, and deal with them in the most excellent manner.

> "But none is granted it except those who are
> patient, and none is granted it except one
> having a great portion (of good)."
> (Surah Fussilat, verse 35)

When the angels open the gate of Jannah for you and give salam to you because you were patience in this life, that is your abode. No change.

> "And We made from among them leaders
> guiding by Our command when they were
> patient and (when) they were certain of Our
> signs." (Surah As-Sajdah, verse 24)

From the verse above, Ibn Al-Qayyim *(may Allah has mercy upon him)* says, "Allah s.w.t has given you two attributes. 'We made among them leaders' when they have patience. And 'they have concrete knowledge of Our signs'. These are the two anecdotes of the two biggest ailments, which is desire and doubt. You have to counter your desires with patience. And you deal with your doubt or ignorance of the religion with knowledge."

Imam Ahmad ibn Hanbal *(may Allah has mercy upon him)* said that sabr or patience was mentioned 90 times in the Quran. Your faith is patience about everything that are mentioned – the commands of Allah, the provisions, divine decree, the tests. He said if that is the case, with the emphasis of patience and since the proof your iman is patience; then human being is created to go to Jannah.

One time, Umar ibn Al-Khattab *(may Allah be pleased with him)* was asked, "How do you handle patience?"

He said, "Alhamdulillah, my test is not in my deen. It could have been worse. Allah is with the patience if they are patient. Indeed, Allah loves those who are patient."

When it comes to the affairs of this worldly life, look at those who are less than you. You will be grateful. But when it comes to the affairs of the religion, look at the ones who is better than you and try to compete with that and excel.

The scholars say if the only verse in the Quran is that as the reward of patience, it would be sufficient.

"... Indeed, the patient will be given their reward without account."
(Surah Az-Zumar, verse 10)

There few opinions on this verse. When everybody else is standing for 50,000 years and they are drenched in sweat, when people will run away from everyone; Allah s.w.t will grant you Jannah with no accountability. The other opinion says Allah s.w.t will grant you so much reward without being counting how much He is giving you.

Isn't that enough for you when Allah s.w.t says "Be patient" when everybody is in haram relationship and you are not, when everybody is drinking alcohol and you are holding back. What about when everybody else that is doing everything else and you are a human being too, you want to do it but you are holding back. Isn't that enough reward? When everybody else is chasing the love of this worldly life and we are looking for the love of the hereafter, which one is better for you?

> "... Indeed, the patient will be given their reward without account."
> (Surah Az-Zumar, verse 10)

PROPHET MUHAMMAD S.A.W SAID,

"HOW WONDERFUL IS THE AFFAIR OF THE BELIEVER, FOR HIS AFFAIRS ARE ALL GOOD. AND THIS APPLIES TO NO ONE BUT THE BELIEVER. IF SOMETHING GOOD HAPPENS TO HIM, HE IS THANKFUL FOR IT AND THAT IS GOOD FOR HIM. IF SOMETHING BAD HAPPENS TO HIM, HE BEARS IT WITH PATIENCE AND THAT IS GOOD FOR HIM."
(RECORDED BY IMAM MUSLIM)

05

The Awaken Heart

Imagine yourself on a plane and you are taking out your phone, then you look at the photos in your phone gallery and certain contacts, and then you are making yourself beautiful before you land, you put your perfume on because you are going to see your significant other, and all of the sudden: turbulence comes. What do you do? Immediately, you seek forgiveness of Allah!

At that time suddenly you can see a playback of your whole life memories and you think of all the sins you committed and you want to stay away from it and you want to repent. As soon as the plane goes back to normal, what do you do? You become the same person again!

Individuals are very smart. They look at the truth about this life and they realize that is not right. Indeed, the hereafter is the true life. So they took the righteous deeds as the safety book and they crossed it. That's it.

People are in the state of heedlessness. What does that mean? We always find excuses not to do the act of obedience or to delay the worship of Allah. We do not heed to the calls to pray, to wear headscarf, to avoid alcohol, to stay away from bad deeds, to be truthful, and others. We give excuses to change by saying we will do so after we reach 40 years old, for example; or after we get married; or after we perform hajj. No one is guaranteed that. Therefore, we are all asleep or heedless. We are submersed in our own desires and the likes.

When we die, we will become alert. Why? Once you died, the veil is lifted and you can see the truth. You can see angels and what is going on – the things that we do not see now. And when you are in the state of alert, you have a remorse. But the remorse will not help you out of death.

Thus, it is important to have your heart awaken before it is too late. If you are among those who get back to the straight path before it is too late, you will be prosperous in this life and in the hereafter.

You were actually in the state of heedlessness before this. When you see the truth, you realize it is not happening here. Look at Umar ibn Al-Khattab *(may Allah be pleased with him)*. He was stabbed while he was praying, then he fell unconscious. When he woke up, he would ask, "Did you pray?" That was his concern. Can you imagine when you were stabbed and you were going to die and your only concern at that time was whether your people had prayed or not? MashaAllah.

When Sufyan ibn Ath-Thauri *(may Allah have mercy upon him)* was dying, he cried and said that it was because he was feared of his bad ending. Just imagine now, some of the greatest scholars like him are afraid of bad ending. So how are we doing? Do we care at all about our ending?

Even Prophet Muhammad s.a.w said he did not know what will be his end. He wanted to relay the message to his people to not seal or feel guaranteed that you will end up in Jannah. No one is guaranteed.

Abu Bakar As-Siddiq *(may Allah be pleased with him)* said, "Even if I have one foot in Jannah, I will not guarantee myself that I am in Jannah."

We have to wake up before it is too late. Keep reminding yourself what if this is my last blink of eye?

Allah s.w.t says,

"… they are like livestock, rather they are (even) more astray …" (Surah Al-Furqan, verse 44)

Those people are heedless and they are like cattle, but they are actually more led astray. They are so far away from the map, no one knows what they are doing.

"... and there will appear to them from Allah
that which they had not taken into account."
(Surah Az-Zumar, verse 47)

They did not think what is going to happen. Now when that time comes, you will see what you did not have in mind.

"... and do not obey one whose heart We have
made heedless of Our remembrance and who
follow his desire and whose affair is ever (in)
neglect."
(Surah Al-Kahf, verse 28)

Even Allah s.w.t reminds the best of creation, Prophet Muhammad s.a.w, do not follow those who are heedless, those who follow their desires and the heart is led astray.

"And keep yourself patient (by being) with those who call upon their Lord in the morning and the evening ..."
(Surah Al-Kahf, verse 28)

This is the type of people you want to hold on to. These people remember Allah during the day and the night. So ask yourself, what type of company I have.

Do you want to seek the pleasure of Allah and the reward with everything you say, you do, you see, you hear, and everything in your life? Do you want Jannah with that? Or in whatever that you do, do you instead seek the wrath of Allah and the Hellfire?

Some of the righteous people have said, "By Allah, I have never took a step in my life or done anything in my life without saying or thinking is this going to take me to heaven or is this going to take me to Hellfire?"

Tell yourself: "I need to wake up now because this is the best time to wake up." So when that happens, think about it. What is the measuring stick that you have for yourself. Because on the Day of Judgment, you will see as if you have nothing. This whole life was just a day or a night.

Allah s.w.t has given you so many examples. In the story of Yusuf (a.s), when did his brothers wake up? When they had done to them what they done to others. When their young brother was taken away, they immediately woken up. What would they going to tell their father?

It is the sign of mercy of Allah s.w.t that He will give you a taste of punishment in this life before the hereafter, because you cannot withstand it there. It is a sign of mercy of Allah s.w.t that He wakes you up a little bit. So that maybe we will come back to the straight path.

For example, you may have a car accident, or you may lose a beloved ones, and you think it is bad when that could be the best thing ever happens to you. Maybe Allah s.w.t will open the gates for you for your reactions and deeds, and closes the gates of acceptance because you are not sincere. Then He will test you with the sin, so you can wake up and you repent and come back to Him.

If you gain Allah s.w.t, it does not matter what you lose. But if you lose Allah s.w.t, it does not matter what you gain. So wake up and gain Allah s.w.t. Take the straight path, go back in the footsteps of Rasulullah s.a.w, take the Quran and sunnah, take the righteous company, stay in the righteous environment, do not worry about what you lost in the process because this is the best gain in this life.

Think about the stories we have read above and also what happens after you get awaken. And this is another story for us to reflect on.

In one whole university, there is one sister who dons headscarf everyday. One of the non-Muslim professor in that university said, "I saw this girl so committed, so I said she deserves my respect and attention. I have to help her." By the grace of Allah, this professor is now a Muslim.

Indeed, Allah s.w.t protects and defends those who believe. People will respect you because everybody else would do whatever it is while you are hanging on to your identity. You will be known and you will not be harmed. By the example of the above story, can you imagine you being the reason for somebody to become a Muslim? It is because of your deeds and you walk on that straight path.

In surah Fatir, verse 37, Allah s.w.t says,

"But did We not grant you life enough for
whoever would remember therein to remember,
and the warner had come to you?"

There are different opinions on the interpretations of the warner in this verse. It is either Prophet Muhammad s.a.w or different ones. When you do a janaza and you do not believe in that as the warner yourself, you may look at the signs or the lines that you have on your eyes, look at yourself in the mirror – you will see certain things is not there anymore; you cannot see without a glass, you cannot hear without hearing aid, and certain things that you can do before but no more now. Isn't that considered as a warner?

We claim that we want to go to Jannah, but we do not do anything to help us to get there. We claim that we want to stay away from Hellfire, but we do not do anything to keep us away from that. We know that Allah s.w.t gives us life, but we worship somebody else. We know that Allah s.w.t gives us the Quran, but we do not follow it. We claim that Prophet

Muhammad s.a.w is our role model, but we do not follow his sunnah. We see janaza but we do not learn from it. Wake up before it is too late.

> "And who is more unjust than one who is reminded of the verses of his Lord but turns away from them and forgets what his hands have put forth? ..."
> (Surah Al-Kahf, verse 57)

Even Prophet Muhammad s.a.w made this dua: *Allahumma inni a'udhubika min zawali ni'matik, wa tahawwuli 'afiyatik, wa fuja-ati nikmatik, wa jami'i sakhatik.* O Allah, I seek refuge in You from the decline of Your blessings, and the removal of our state of well-being, and the sudden onset of Your punishment, and from all that displeases You. (Recorded in Sahih Muslim)

The most important blessing is Islam. Those who say "My Lord is Allah" and then they stay on the straight path, the angels come down upon these people and give them good news, "Do not be afraid and do not be sad." Usually we are afraid of our future. We do not know what will happen. And we feel sad about the sins that we have done. Do not be afraid about the future and do not be sad about the past.

Just remember to take advantage of five before five: your health before your illness, your wealth before your poverty, your young age before your old age, your time before you lose your time, and your life before your death. Do not be heedless of these blessings that Allah s.w.t has bestowed upon you.

Understand that whatever happens to you in this life is good. It is because Allah s.w.t wants to wake you up. He does not want you to go to Hellfire. So help yourself.

"... and do not be among the heedless." (Surah Al-A'raf, verse 205)

Prophet Muhammad s.a.w said, "What I told you to do, do it as much as you can. What I told you to stay away from, stay away from it." He did not give an option here. So when in the above verse, Allah s.w.t said do not be among the heedless, heed to the order.

"Indeed in that is a sign for those who fear the
punishment of the hereafter ..."
(Surah Hud, verse 103)

Everything that you see here is the awaken or a sign
for those who want to protect themselves from the
punishment in the akhirah life.

"Indeed you are only a warner for those who
fear it."
(Surah An-Nazi'at, verse 45)

Allah s.w.t says, "Indeed, o Messenger of Allah, you are
mere a warner for those who are fearing and conscious
of the Hellfire and the truth of the hereafter."

When you are standing drenched in your sweat
on the Day of Judgment, is that the only time you
are going to wake up? Or imagine when the Angel of
Death is coming to you; what are you going to do?

Remind yourself with the Quran if you fear that
time and you long to go to Jannah. Stay away from
Hellfire.

IF YOU GAIN ALLAH S.W.T, IT DOES NOT MATTER WHAT YOU LOSE. BUT IF YOU LOSE ALLAH S.W.T, IT DOES NOT MATTER WHAT YOU GAIN.

Istiqamah

The definition of istiqamah is being steadfast on the straight path. It is path that Allah s.w.t paved for us. We ask Allah for that seventeen times a day.

"Guide us to the straight path."
(Surah Al-Fatihah, verse 6)

Allah s.w.t gives us a way; a GPS how to get there in this life and in the hereafter. And then we ask Allah in the dua.

"The path of those upon whom You have bestowed favor, not of those who have evoked (Your) anger or of those who are astray."
(Surah Al-Fatihah, verse 7)

Islam is a blessing in itself. The biggest blessing that we take for granted is that saying "La ilaha illa Allah, Muhammadur Rasulullah." Straight path is also a blessing from Allah s.w.t. That is why Ibn Al-Qayyim *(may Allah has mercy upon him)* said, "The best honor that Allah bestowed upon you is holding on to the straight path."

When Allah s.w.t gives you the blessing of knowledge and you do not follow, then you deserve the wrath of Allah. But if the door of actions and deeds are open for you and you do not do according to the straight path – a guidance from Allah in the Quran and the tradition of the Messenger of Allah s.a.w – then you are being led astray.

Umar ibn Al-Khattab *(may Allah be pleased with him)* said, "If you want to pray, pray. If you want to fast, fast. But be steadfast on the straight path." Because you can fast the wrong way or pray the wrong way if you do not do it with sincerity, or you do it not according to the sunnah.

For those who have business, what is the measure whether you are successful or not? It is through your profit and loss record. Similarly, in the deen, the measure is the istiqamah. On the Day of Judgment, you will get your Balance Sheet. It is the record of your good deeds and sins.

When we say "Guide us to the straight path", the scholars say that the straigth path is to follow the Quran and the sunnah. If you want to be guided, hold on to the Quran and the sunnah.

Some of us would say, "If Allah s.w.t wants me to be guided, He will guide me. If He doesn't want me to be guided, I'm not going to do something." Blaming Allah s.w.t for your miseries or for your own sins is a hopeless denial statement.

Allah s.w.t ordains everything that is good and forbade everything that is bad. When a man drank alcohol and he said, "This is qadr of Allah unto me", Umar ibn Al-Khattab *(may Allah be pleased with him)* said, "Establish the penalty upon this man twice. First, because he drank alcohol. Second, because he is lying upon Allah s.w.t."

What is the straight path? It is the shortest distance between the two points. Thus, if you want the shortest distance to Allah s.w.t, the road map is clear. It is so easy as we have the technology. However, if you go to the right of it or to the left a bit, that means it is a triangle now and you have lost a bit of distance. Same thing when it goes up and down.

Prophet Muhammad s.a.w said, "Hold on to the straight path. You will not be able to attain it perfectly." (Hadith sahih Al-Albani) It is impossible. To be able to give Allah s.w.t what He deserves is impossible. But still, do your best.

Allah s.w.t gives command to Prophet Muhammad s.a.w, "Be straight therein." The Prophet s.a.w said this verse made his hair turned grey early. But Allah s.w.t said it is only by the blessings of Allah that He gives him the ability to be steadfast on this path.

After every salah – obligatory or voluntarily – recite this dua: *Allahumma a'inni 'ala dhikrika wa shukrika wa husni 'ibadatik.* This is the dua that Prophet Muhammad s.a.w taught Mu'adh ibn Jabal. The Prophet s.a.w said to Mu'adh, "O Mu'adh, I love you and because of that I am teaching you this dua."

Ibn Uthaymeen *(may Allah has mercy upon him)* said, "Recite this dua before you go to sleep." This is probably the strongest opinion on the time to recite this dua.

On the straight path, you can see the bigger picture and bigger goal. However, you will get distracted with very minor things; kids, spouse, job, politics, economy, and others. You are submersed in this worldly life but you are not looking at your hereafter. The hereafter is the bigger thing. If you focus on this bigger thing, anything that is bothering you in this worldly life can be easily ignored or you will pay just a little attention to it. You will say, "It's only life." Whether people are going to be happy with you or not, it does not matter to you for as long as Allah s.w.t is happy with you.

If you hold on to the straight path, you will get all the beautiful provisions. On the contrary, if you turn your back physically and also your heart away from Allah s.w.t, you are going to have a tough life both in this world and in the hereafter. It does not matter how much money you have in the bank, it does not matter how many people like your social media updates; there is a void. Because when you are alone, you know you are not on the straight path. You are afraid to die. If you are not on the straight path in this worldly life, you are not going to be on the straight path in the hereafter.

In surah Al-An'am, verse 153, Allah s.w.t says,

> "And (moreover) this is My path, which is straight, so follow it ..."

But when Allah talks about the different path, He says, "And do not follow the different paths and it will take you away from His path." The straight path is mentioned as a singular path, while the different paths are mentioned as plural paths. More than one path. And the shaytan will take you away from the straight path one step at a time.

How does shaytan take you from the straight path? From four directions; from the front, from the back, from the right, and from the left. But he did not mention two directions: up and down. From the front, shaytan will lure you with attachment and attention of the worldly life and of the future. From the back, he will make you despair in Allah's mercy. From the right, he will make you feel doubt about good deeds. And from the left, he will make you feel doubt about the negative effect of bad deeds.

How is it then you end up be following the straight path and the different paths? People follow the different paths when they do not believe in the hereafter, when they stay away from the active acts of obedience. Therefore, iman on the straight path and holding on to it is a blessing that Allah s.w.t bestowed upon you.

A man came to Prophet Muhammad s.a.w and said, "Give me an advice. I will not ask anyone else."

The Prophet s.a.w replied, "Say 'I believe in Allah' then be steadfast on this straight path."

One of the interpretations on 'I believe in Allah' is that it is a declaration. Do not be afraid to declare your faith to others. Being on the straight path is the best form of dawah. Saying 'I believe in Allah' is something we call as aqeedah. What is the proof of this aqeedah? By doing righteous deeds.

> "Among the believers are men true to what they promised Allah ..."
> (Surah Al-Ahzab, verse 23.)

These people in the above verse rush to Allah s.w.t because they want to hold that reward of the hereafter for that promise they made with Allah. Do not betray the promised made with Allah s.w.t, do not betray the Messenger of Allah s.a.w, do not betray the Quran, do not betray the sunnah; because if you do, that is how you are going to betray yourself eventually.

How do you know that you are on the straight path? If you know you are really on the straight path, if I tell you that tomorrow is the Day of Judgment, you will not be able to increase the act of obedience.

"Indeed, those who have said, 'Our Lord is
Allah' and then remained on the right course,
the angels will descend upon them (saying),
'Do not fear and do not grieve but receive good
tidings of Paradise, which you were promised.'"
(Surah Fussilat, verse 30)

This is the verse that hopefully will get you to the straight path. Allah s.w.t gives this beautiful glad tiding to those who held themselves on the straight path – perform the acts of obedience and leave the acts of disobedience, held on to the righteous environment and the righteous company even though it is difficult.

It is time for us to wake up and say "Our Lord is Allah s.w.t". Our lord is not the dollar and cents. Our lord is not the boss, nor the spouse, nor the children, nor our desires, nor the worldly life.

"Have you seen the one who takes as his god his
own desire? ..."
(Surah Al-Furqan, verse 43)

Those who said "Our Lord is Allah", then the proof
for saying that is not a lip service, but rather in the
righteous deeds. The scholars said that the angels
mentioned in verse 30 surah Fussilat is the angels that
descend upon you when you die. Because when you
die, you can see the Angels of Punishment or Angels of
Mercy. Which angels that you will see depends on what
your investment while you are alive. Did you invest
more on good deeds or more on bad deeds. Was your
investment being done more on the straight path or the
different paths?

WHEN YOU DIE, YOU CAN SEE THE ANGELS OF PUNISHMENT OR ANGELS OF MERCY. WHICH ANGELS THAT YOU WILL SEE DEPENDS ON WHAT YOUR INVESTMENT WHILE YOU ARE ALIVE. DID YOU INVEST MORE ON GOOD DEEDS OR MORE ON BAD DEEDS. WAS YOUR INVESTMENT BEING DONE MORE ON THE STRAIGHT PATH OR THE DIFFERENT PATHS?

07

Muraqabah

The definition of muraqabah is you know that Allah s.w.t sees you and you are certain that Allah s.w.t is with you and that He knows your hidden secrets and your apparent affairs, and continuity of consistency of knowing that knowledge till the last day of your life.

Think of this. You are going to record an episode as a news anchor. Before the recording starts, you and the people behind the scene are busy with makeup and wardrobe and anything that needs touch-up. As soon as the red light on the camera is on, you cannot do all that because you are on air. You have to be very careful of what you say, how you act, what you do.

That is exactly the same feeling I want you to attain at all times. Allah s.w.t is with you. He can see you and hear you all the time. The companions (may Allah be pleased with all of them) used to teach their children three things: Allah sees me, Allah watches over me, and Allah is with me.

So if you know that for sure, you can never go wrong. If I give you a Go-Pro and it is mounted on your forehead and you are free to do whatever you want today, but tomorrow we are going to download everything that you have seen, heard, been to on that day and we are going to review it in front of everyone; can you imagine? What will you do? What will you see? What will you hear? Where will you go? That is exactly the muraqabah.

That is why if you know that somebody is watching over you from the human beings, you are going to get tired. You do not want people to watch you. But if you know that Allah s.w.t is with you, watches over you, protects you, and so on; you could never have anything better than that. That is the difficult difference between the hypocrite and the believer.

The highest level of iman is that you know that Allah s.w.t watches over you, and He is with you and protects you, He can hear you, He can be with you all the time. And know for sure that Allah s.w.t does not just know what you do; He knows what is inside of you – your secrets. So be conscious of Him and be careful. Indeed, Allah s.w.t watches over everything.

> "Does he not know that Allah sees?"
> (Surah Al-'Alaq, verse 14)

There is a story of a man with three children and he was going to die. He took the three children and said, "I want to pick a leader among you, but I don't know which one is the one." He gave to each of them a chicken and said, "Go slaughter it in a place where no one will see you." Two of the children came back with a chicken slaughtered. The youngest one came back with the chicken alive. The man asked them, "Didn't I tell you to slaughter the chicken?" The youngest child said, "Yes, Dad. But you said do it at a place that Allah s.w.t does not see you. Everywhere I went I was sure that Allah s.w.t can see me." Even though he is the youngest among the three children, the man chose him to be the leader. He said, "You are the Ameer! After I go, you become the Ameer." How could not be?

Know that Allah s.w.t sees the dark, black end, in the dark night, under a solid rock. So how could He not know who you are, what you do, what you see, and what you hear?

Be conscious of Allah s.w.t and make sure you make your secret life is better than your public life. Zubayr ibn Awwam *(may Allah be pleased with him)* said, "Do have secret good deeds like you have secret bad deeds."

We know that everybody has secrets and perhaps hidden sins that we do not want others to know – but Allah knows about it. What Zubayr ibn Awwam is saying is that just like you want to keep something bad about you from others - although Allah s.w.t knows – do at least keep an amount of good deeds that only you and Allah s.w.t know and that no one else knows.

Zayn Al-Abideen *(may Allah be pleased with him)* used to help people by giving food for them at night. No one saw him. They only found out when he died. How did they find out? The food was cut off. When they were washing his body, they saw black line on his back where he used to carry the foods.

Know for sure that the secret sins will destroy you. And the secret good deeds are the one that will actually save you.

In surah Al-Hadid, verse 4 Allah s.w.t says,

"… and He is with you wherever you are; and
Allah, of what you do is Seeing."

What is ihsaan? In Sahih al-Bukhari, Abu Huraira narrated: One day while the Messenger of Allah was sitting with the people, a man came to him walking and said, "O Messenger of Allah, what is belief?" The Prophet said, "Belief is to believe in Allah, His angels, His books, His messengers, and the meeting with Him, and to believe in the resurrection." The man asked, "O Messenger of Allah, what is Islam?" The Prophet replied, "Islam is to worship Allah and not worship anything besides Him, to offer prayers perfectly, to pay the (compulsory) charity – zakat – and to fast the month of Ramadan." The man again asked, "O Messenger of Allah, what is ihsaan?" The Prophet said, "Ihsaan is to worship Allah as if you see him, and if you do not achieve this state of devotion, then (take it for granted that) Allah sees you." The man further asked, "O Messenger of Allah, when will the hour be established?" The Prophet said, "The one who is asked about it does not know more than the questioner does, but I will describe to you its portents. When the lady slave gives birth to her mistress, that will be of its portents; when the barefooted naked people become the chiefs of the people, that will be of its portents. The Hour is one of five things which nobody knows except Allah. Verily, the knowledge of the Hour is with Allah (alone). He sends down the rain, and knows that which is in the wombs." Then the man left. The Prophet said, "Call him back to me." They went to call him back but could not see him. The Prophet said, "That was Jibril who came to teach the people their religion."

Ihsaan is not to be good to those who are good towards you. Ihsaan is to be good to those who are bad towards you.

In Sunan Ibn Majah, it was narrated from Ibn Thawban that the Prophet s.a.w said, "I certainly know people of my nation who will come on the Day of Resurrection with good deeds like the mountains of Tihamah, but Allah will make them like scattered dust." Thawban said, "O Messenger of Allah, describe them to us and tell us more, so that we will not become of them unknowingly." He said, "They are your brothers and from your race, worshiping at night as you do, but they will be people who, when they are alone, transgress the sacred limit of Allah." This hadith is graded as hasan.

Do not let Allah s.w.t be the least of your worries of those who see you. All the salawat that you did, all the fasting, zakat, sadaqah, hajj, umrah, lowering the gaze, patience in difficulties; all of that you have been through will be gone. Why? Because when you are alone, you do not conscious of Allah s.w.t. There is no muraqabah.

The signs to know that we are aware of Allah s.w.t sees us.

1.   Selflessness in a way that you put whatever Allah s.w.t bestowed upon us before anything else. The love of Allah s.w.t before the love of your desires. Allah s.w.t comes before anything else. Islam comes before anything else. Muslims come before anybody else. What Allah loves for us to do comes before what we want to do.

2.   Glorifying what Allah s.w.t glorified and belittling what Allah s.w.t belittled.

These are some measuring sticks you have to remember. How do you do that? With the names and attributes of Allah. Among the names and attributes of Allah is Al-Hafiz, Ar-Raqeeb, Al-'Adhim, As-Sami', and Al-Basir.

On the Day of Judgment, when we deny anything that is presented to us, we will be shown the proof because everything is recorded. Allah s.w.t is Ar-Raqeeb. He watches over us. Everything is copied.

Allah is Al-'Aleem. He knows everything. He is As-Sami', He hears everything. Allah is Al-Basir, He sees everything. So if you have the names and attributes of Allah and know what it means, you will be on the straight path.

Allah s.w.t says,

"They conceal from the people, but they cannot conceal from Allah ..."
(Surah An-Nisa, verse 108)

You are bashful and you are hiding from people, but you are not bashful and hiding from Allah s.w.t. Where are you going to run? On the Day of Judgment when Allah s.w.t say, "Run back to Allah!" There is no mountain you can hide behind. There is no hole you can run into. There is no tribe who can protect you. There is no money you can bribe the angels.

"And you were not covering yourselves, lest
your hearing testify against you or your sight or
your skins, but you assumed that Allah does not
know much of what you do."
(Surah Fussilat, verse 22)

You do not know the fact that your vision will testify against you, your hearing will testify against you, and even the skin will testify against you. That is why it is mentioned that Allah s.w.t will renew the skin. On the Day of Judgment, everything else will talk on your behalf; will testify for you or against you.

Imagine you are going to the mall and you want something so bad, but you do not have the money. Still, you walk-in to the shop and you see the warning "Shoplifting will be prosecuted". Then you hold back. But then shaytan comes and give you waswasa. He whispers to you, "You can do it, man!" Then you go inside again. When you look around, there is a camera everywhere. Then you find a place where the camera position is not that apparent. So you grab that thing that you really want, thinking you can get away with it. Just on the way out, somebody grabs your hand. What are you going to do when they come for you?

Think that the security guard that grabs your hand just before you go as the Angel of Death. What happens? You know that people who pay so much money for you to come to overseas to get your

Ph.D? Everyone works so hard to get the money and everybody else is waiting for you to come back and save the country and the world. Now your photo will be on the front page, but instead of the news that says "Dr. Fulan, a Successful and Righteous …" like everybody thought it would be, it says "Dr. Fulan, a Criminal …" Can you imagine that?

A scholar was asked, "How do a slave of Allah attains Jannah?" These are his answers.

1. Be steadfast without wavering.

2. Strive without heedlessness.

3. Be conscious of Allah s.w.t, who watches over you in secret and public life.

Make your private life better than your public life. If you even conscious of Allah s.w.t in your thoughts, Allah will repair and protect your senses.

Ibn Al-Qayyim *(may Allah has mercy on him)* give additional answers to the list above.

4. Waiting for death and preparing for it.

5. Holding yourself accountable before you are counted on.

There was a righteous young boy and he was hungry. He was looking for an apple and it fell in front of him. So he ate it. After his hunger was gone, he became conscious again. "Oh my God, I did not know where this apple came from. And I didn't ask permission from the garden's owner." Then he found out who the owner of the garden is.

When he saw the owner, he said, "Sir, I took an apple without your permission."

The man could not believe it. A young man traveled far to apologize for an apple! Who among us would do that? The owner said, "I will not forgive you."

The young man said, "Please forgive me. I will do anything."

The owner said, "The only way I'm going to forgive you is you have to marry my daughter."

The young man asked, "Is there anything else I have to do?"

The owner said, "No, that is the only way I will forgive you. But before you say yes, I have to tell you. She cannot see, cannot hear, cannot talk, and cannot walk."

The young man said, "I accept."

After he accepted, a beautiful girl came walking through the door. She said, "Assalamualaikum."

The young man said to the owner, "You lied to me."

The owner asked, "What do you mean?"

The young man continued, "You told me she doesn't see, doesn't talk, and all."

The owner replied, "I did not lie to you. What I meant when I said she doesn't see is she doesn't see haram. When I told you she cannot hear, it means she cannot hear haram. When I said she cannot talk, I meant she cannot talk haram. When I told you she cannot walk, it means she doesn't walk to the places that are haram."

Umar ibn Al-Khattab *(may Allah be pleased with him)* was walking in the night and then he heard a young daughter talking to her mother. The mother asked her daughter to mix the milk with water. Cut the long story, Umar ibn Al-Khattab knocked on the door. Then he said, "Fear Allah!"

Then he went back and he came again. He heard the mother said the same thing to her daughter – to add water to the milk. The young daughter said, "Didn't Amirul Mukminin Umar Al-Khattab told us not to do that?"

The mother said, "Where is Umar now?"

The young daughter replied, "And where is the Lord of Umar?"

Umar *(may Allah be pleased with him)* was so impressed. Then he ran home and said, "One of you, my sons, must marry this girl. If none of you marry her, I will." So one of his sons marry the young daughter. The lineage of that marriage was Umar ibn Abdul 'Aziz *(may Allah be pleased with him)*.

Every time you are alone, ask yourself, "Where is Allah?" Every time you want to do something haram, ask yourself, "Where is Allah?" Every time you want to see something haram, ask yourself, "Where is Allah?" Every time you want to go to a place that is haram, ask yourself, "Where is Allah?"

One time, one of the righteous men said, "Before I do anything, I take two measure sticks. Before I do any thing, I remind myself with this verse from the Quran,

> But for he who has feared the position of his
> Lord are two gardens-'"
> (Surah Ar-Rahman, verse 46)

And then he also said, "Before I do anything, I ask myself,

> Is this better or the Garden of Eternity which is
> promised to the righteous?
> (Surah Al-Furqan, verse 15)"

Hold on to muraqabah as if your life depends on it.

THE COMPANIONS
(MAY ALLAH BE PLEASED
WITH ALL OF THEM)
USED TO TEACH THEIR
CHILDREN THREE THINGS:
ALLAH SEES ME, ALLAH
WATCHES OVER ME, AND
ALLAH IS WITH ME.

08

Accountability (Muhasabah)

Accountability is you differentiate between what is requested or required or asked of you and what is that which belongs to you. You do what is asked of you and you give or you take what is that is yours. This is a very simple accountability of plus and minus.

Umar ibn Al-Khattab *(may Allah be pleased with him)* used to say, "Hold yourself accountable before you are held accountable and weigh your actions before they are weighed on you. Know for sure that the Angel of Death now has somebody to go to or he passed you to go to somebody else. And tomorrow, they will pass everybody to come to you."

What do you have to do? You have to understand that if you love or you long to see Allah s.w.t, He will love to meet you too. But if you abhor or dislike meeting with Allah s.w.t, He will treat you the same. So how do you do that? Most of us actually hate death. Even 'Aisha *(may Allah be pleased with her)* asked The Prophet s.a.w about death.

Prophet Muhammad s.a.w said, "It is not that, 'Aisha. It is when you do righteous deeds, you look forward to your reward for what you sow in this life. So you look forward to meeting Allah s.w.t. Hence,

Allah s.w.t loves to meet you. But if you don't do righteous deeds, you don't look forward to the Day of Judgment. Because you know where you are going to end. So you don't look forward to that and Allah s.w.t doesn't look forward to meeting you either."

This matter is totally up to you. Whether you prepare yourself or not prepare yourself. But again, think about the accountability part. You will be studying all year and you go to sleep at the time of exam. You know you have been working hard, you know that you are going to get an A+, but the report card is not coming out very well.

However, this is not just about getting a report card. This is heaven and hell. Understand that this is going to be among the days and the nights.

The scholars say there are two nights and two days that you have to worry about. One is the night after you are going to be spending the night in the grave. The other night is the night which after that is the hereafter. Meanwhile, the first day is when Allah s.w.t will come and hold you accountable and the second day is when you are going to get the book of accountability.

Rush in that which Allah s.w.t is pleased with. For example, Umar ibn Al-Khattab *(may Allah be pleased with him)* used to compete with Abu Bakar As-Siddiq *(may Allah be pleased with him)* in doing righteous deeds. If you look at the people of the worldly life, you want to look at the one lesser than you. But in the acts of worship, you look at someone who is better than you.

Abu Hurairah *(may Allah be pleased with him)* cried one night. He was asked, "Why are you crying, o Abu Hurairah?" He replied, "The journey is long but my sustenance of what I need on this journey is very little."

Abdullah ibn Sa'ud *(may Allah be pleased with him)* said, "By Allah, on the Day of Judgment you will be reviewed with every verses in the Quran. The verses that say "Do not do that", the verse will ask you, "Did you stay away from that?" And the verses that told you to do that, the verse will say, "Did you do that?"

In surah Al-Hashr, verse 18, Allah s.w.t says,

"O you who have believed, fear Allah and let every soul look to what it has put forth for tomorrow ..."

Look at what you have sown in this worldly life, what you have done that you will be held accountable for. Remember you love the castles but you forget the grave, you love the creation but you forget the Creator. You have to hold yourself accountable accordingly, because Allah s.w.t says to look forward to what you will be accountable for. But you have to plant it now. The seed of taqwa, the seed of iman, the seed of sadaqah, the seed of salah, the seed of truthfulness, the seed of lowering your gaze, the seed of righteous company and environment, the seed of saying no to drugs and alcohol, and so on.

In surah Al-Infitar, verse 6 Allah s.w.t says,

"O mankind, what has deceived you concerning your Lord, the Generous."

If your own power deceives you to oppress others, remember the power of Allah s.w.t over you.

"O mankind, indeed you are laboring toward your Lord with (great) exertion and will meet it."
(Surah Al-Inshiqaq, verse 6)

You are going to face difficulties in this life, but indeed in the end you are going to meet Allah s.w.t. We will be resurrected and accountable. That is what the Day of Judgment is all about. A true believer looks forward to the true infinite justice on that day.

> "O mankind, indeed the promise of Allah is truth, so let not the worldly life delude you ..."
> (Surah Fatir, verse 5)

Do not be deceived by this life. Most of us have been deceived. What were we deceived by?

> "Competition in (worldly) increase diverts you.
> Until you visit the graveyards."
> (Surah At-Takathur, verses 1-2)

The anguish of death will come with the truth. What is the truth? The truth is that you will die. And the truth is that you will be there. The truth is that you will be resurrected. The truth is that you will hear your name. The truth is that there is no life after death, except Paradise or Hellfire. And the truth is that you know no one will come to your aid. The truth is that you will be going to heaven or hell. The truth is you cannot come back to this life. The truth is you are on your own.

So if you look at the Quran and you look at the lenses of the muhasabah, holding yourself accountable before you are held accountable, it will help you. Because if you hold yourself accountable with great difficulties – with every little thing – it will help you to stay on the straight path.

On the Day of Judgment, there are people who say, "Woe to me and that which I have neglected." So be conscious of Allah in a way that befits His Majesty, although there is no way we can reach that. Even the angels which have been in the position of bow down and prostration since they were created, on the Day of Judgment, they will say "Subhanaka … subhanaka … we have not worship You in the way befitting Your Majesty."

Umar ibn Abdul 'Aziz *(may Allah be pleased with him)* cried one night and he made his whole family cried with him, because of one verse.

"… a party will be in Paradise and a party in the Blaze." (Surah Ash-Shuraa, verse 7)

There is a group of people that will be going to Paradise and another group that will go to the Hellfire.

Some of those who know Allah s.w.t say, "If you think that you are doing whatever you are doing that you pleased with, and then you content with that, then know for sure that Allah s.w.t does not please with you." If you really look into the acts of worship, look at yourself showing off and look at every aspects of it – is it a good dawah for people? And everything that you want in your heart is nothing in comparison to Paradise.

Prophet Muhammad s.a.w said to Mu'adh, "O Mu'adh, do you know what are the rights upon Allah? It is to worship Him and do not ascribe partners onto Him. And what are the rights now for the slaves? He (Allah) should not punish them." So we must live and die upon *La ilaha illa Allah, Muhammadun rasulullah.*

The next story took place somewhere close to Makkah. There were three real estate agents. The owner did not know the value of his place and it is a valuable land. The three real estate agents who are partners bought that piece of land which supposed to be very expensive, but they were not fair with the owner. They paid him very little money. When the man finally realized about this matter, he was not happy. However, look at how Allah s.w.t held the three agents accountable.

After they took the land, they built a high rise. The first man died while he was trying to climb the wall because he fell. The second man died when a big crane fell on him. The third man realized now what was going on. So he ran right away to the owner of the land. He said, "We did not do you justice. Here is the amount of the money that belongs to you. It is the real value of this land. Please take it."

Allah s.w.t woke him up before he caught up with his two friends.

You have to differentiate between the blessings of Allah s.w.t and condemnation of Allah. For example, you have a handphone and you use it for righteousness; that is a blessing. But if you use it in the wrong way – watching the wrong things, listen to the wrong things, and all of that – that is a form of condemnation.

Prophet Muhammad s.a.w said, "Indeed, what is lawful is very clear and what is unlawful is also very clear. And between them there is a gray area. Those who stay away from the gray area is innocent of anything."

Do not roam around what is haram. Do not ask to be tested as we are not that strong. Do not put yourself in the midst of fitnah and say you can handle it. Leave what that makes you doubt to what does not make you doubt. Lock that door.

The repentance is between two accountability. One, you hold yourself accountable. If that is the case, you will repent. And once you repent, you will hold others accountable. So get that before it is too late.

Ibn Al-Qayyim *(may Allah has mercy on him)* said, "The first thing you want to do is hold yourself accountable. How? Number one, through the obligations. Number two, through what is forbidden. Number three, through the matter of heedlessness. Number four, through your senses."

Ibn Qudamah *(may Allah has mercy on him)* said, "You have to take yourself into six stages.

1. *Musharatah.* Put a condition upon yourself. "If I do this, I better do that."

2. *Muraqabah.* Be conscious that Allah is watching you all the time.

3. *Muhasabah.* You hold yourself accountable for everything that you are doing.

4. *Mu'aqabah.* If there is something wrong, you punish yourself in a way that is halal.

5. *Mujahadah.*

6. *Mu'atabah.*

The whole thing is now how to end up, not how you start.

IBN AL-QAYYIM (MAY ALLAH HAS MERCY ON HIM) SAID, "THE FIRST THING YOU WANT TO DO IS HOLD YOURSELF ACCOUNTABLE. HOW? NUMBER ONE, THROUGH THE OBLIGATIONS. NUMBER TWO, THROUGH WHAT IS FORBIDDEN. NUMBER THREE, THROUGH THE MATTER OF HEEDLESSNESS. NUMBER FOUR, THROUGH YOUR SENSES."

Dependent on Allah

We are dependent on Allah s.w.t. And He is independent of everything. Allah is Self-Sufficient while we are in need of Him.

You should have nothing for your own desires. Everything that you do, say, hear, see are all for Allah s.w.t. That is how we know what we are poor and in need of Allah s.w.t.

> "O mankind, you are those in need of Allah,
> while Allah is free of need, the Praiseworthy."
> (Surah Fatir, verse 15)

> Even Musa a.s in a story mentioned in the Quran,
> he said, "My Lord, indeed I am for whatever good
> You would send down to me, in need."
> (Surah Al-Qasas, verse 24)

Musa a.s is among the five of *ulil 'azm* – the strongest, most persevered prophets of Allah. And he still asked help from Allah s.w.t.

As we mentioned before, our prayers, our rituals, our life, and our death are for Allah alone. How do you do that? What is the condition?

You say that you love Allah s.w.t and everything that you do is for Allah, but when someone asks what are you created for, you will mention the verse that says we are not created to other than worshiping Allah. But that is not the answer. Behind that question is that does your actions and deeds say that you are created to worship Allah? How is it exactly you walk the talk?

Be careful of your secret life because on the Day of Judgment, Allah s.w.t will reveal all the secrets. That means you take out everything of your heart, except Allah s.w.t. You have to understand, outwardly and internally. The actions and deeds are also the sincerity of the heart. Not just the actions of the limbs.

One man walks around and he asks, "You know who I am?"

Someone said, "Yes, I know who you are. You were started with a drop of sperm and you hold filth inside of you and in the end you are going to be corpse and rot."

The man said, "Indeed, you know me."

Walk upon the earth in humbleness as if you can hear the earth saying to you, "O son of Adam, you walk upon me. But after a while, you will walk inside of me. So be careful of what you do above me and I will treat you accordingly inside of me." You come from the back of the earth to the stomach of the earth. And then you will come back again to the destination that is up to you, by the mercy of Allah.

How to obtain this level of dependency in Allah?

1. Understanding who Allah s.w.t and His power.

   Fudayl ibn Iyad *(may Allah be pleased with him)* said, "The most knowledgeable of Allah s.w.t is the most conscious of Allah." Look into the ayatul kursi and ponder upon it.

2. Understanding how weak we are.

   Look at what you were created from. Think about the comparison between life and death and the circle of life.

3. Consistency in remembering Allah and asking Him to forgive us.

Indeed with the remembrance of Allah does the heart find peace and tranquility. When your heart is at peace from the remembrance of Allah, anything that is happening to you, you know that it is only life.

Recite the sayyidul istighfar and ponder upon the meaning. Look at the submission at the beginning of the recitation.

Ibn Al-Qayyim said, "If you are among those people, you will be rich with no wealth, honored even though you have no tribe, and you are feared with no power.

4. You are afraid that your actions and deeds be accepted or not.

'Aisha *(may Allah be pleased with her)* asked the Prophet s.a.w, "Are those the one who do bad deeds?" Prophet Muhammad s.a.w said, "No, 'Aisha. They are the one who fasts and prays, but they are afraid whether Allah is going to accept their actions or not."

5. To be conscious of Allah s.w.t in your secret life and in your public life.

   Those who are conscious of the status of Allah s.w.t and forbade their own desires, for sure their eternal abode is Paradise. Remember Allah sincerely when no one else is around you.

Four things you have to do in order to obtain all of these:

1. Allah s.w.t does not need our actions and deeds.

   In a hadith qudsi, Allah s.w.t says, "You will never reach the status that you will be able to harm me. Nor that you will reach the status that you will benefit Me. But it is your actions and deeds that I will hold to accountable for you."

2. If Allah accepts our actions and deeds, it is only by the blessing of Allah and by His mercy and generosity. Not by anything else.

Prophet Muhammad s.a.w said even he will not enter Paradise with his actions and deeds. It is all by the mercy of Allah s.w.t.

3. Everything that Allah s.w.t has done for us is only by His mercy and we are grateful to Him.

    Allah s.w.t has actually done us favor that we actually say *la ilaha illa Allah, Muhammadan rasulullah.* At least, you should be grateful for this.

4. Do not ever sit back and say that you are done.

    Do not settle yet. Make sure you keep going. Worship your Lord until death comes upon you.

Four pillars of being in need of Allah s.w.t:

1. Knowledge that will keep you on the straight path. The more you acquire knowledge, the more you are conscious of Allah s.w.t.

2. You leave some of the halal fearing that it is haram. Leave that what makes you doubt.

3. Certainty that will carry you to continue on this life, even though it is difficult.

4. Remembering Allah s.w.t all the time in every aspect of your life; in good or bad, standing or sitting, and so on.

If you know the truth about being in need of Allah s.w.t, this is the truth about being rich or self-sufficient. Ali ibn Abi Talib *(may Allah be pleased with him)* was asked who is the rich and who is poor. He said, "You will know whether you are rich or poor after you're reviewed by Allah s.w.t."

" My Lord,
INDEED I AM FOR
WHATEVER GOOD YOU
WOULD SEND DOWN TO
ME, IN NEED. "